WORD
of
HOPE
Devotional

ANGELO BARBOSA

www.xulonpress.com

Preface

WORD OF HOPE

Word of Hope has been compiled with you in mind,
to encourage and enlighten you.

S piritual growth is necessary to fulfill your God-given
purpose and achieve your dreams. This guide will equip
you with the tools you need to change your life and shed
light along your path as you grow. Your transformation will
have a positive impact on those around you, and you will be a
beacon of hope and a channel of truth and love.

With your heart opened to receive more of God, I pray
that *Word of Hope* will expand and bring focus to your vision
of His great plan and purpose for your life. May His grace
encompass you, and may hope rise in your heart and overflow
in your life for His glory and praise. God bless you abundantly.

Bishop Angelo Barbosa

Table of Contents

ALL THINGS WORK TOGETHER...

Once there was an extremely powerful king who had many officials, and among them was a faithful Christian. This man knew God and the power of His resurrection, and stood firm in his walk with the Lord. He was always confident and had a positive outlook on life, no matter what came his way. For this reason, the king was drawn to him. So whenever the king was confronted with a problem, he would seek his counsel. One of his favorite expressions for any situation was, "God is good and all things work together for good to those who love Him." So the king grew to love his God.

It so happened that one day the king had an accident and lost his ring finger. Now, for any king, the ring finger is considered to be very important because it signifies power and authority. So again, he turned to his Christian friend for comfort. As usual, he was told not to worry and that all things work together for good to those who love God. Sad to say, the king did not appreciate that response. He felt insulted and became very upset with the Christian, because he just could not see how losing a finger, the most important finger of all, would work in his favor. So he ordered that this Christian be arrested and put in prison for his insult to the king.

After some time had passed, the king decided to go on a journey with the rest of his top officials. While on that journey, they were attacked by a cannibalistic tribe who bound them and started to kill and eat them, one by one. When they got to the king, the leader of the tribe began to examine him for any form of defect, because this would make him unclean and unworthy to be eaten. When they saw he had a missing finger, they rejected him. He was released and allowed to return to his kingdom. It was at that moment that he remembered the words of his friend: "All things work together for good to those who love God." Had he not lost his finger, his encounter with the cannibals would have been the end of his life. Have we seen how good God is in this story? Alleluia!

Like the king, it is often difficult for us to see good in the tough times we face; but if we love God, He assures us that all things work together for our good. Even the things the devil meant for evil, He will turn it to good. Praise God!

By the way, following the king's return to his kingdom, the Christian was released from prison and promoted to the highest position in the kingdom. So again, we see things working out for his good.

Let's Pray

Dear Lord, help me to see You and Your goodness in every situation in my life, and to give You glory instead of complaining. **Amen.**

CALL UPON HIM

And the Lord said: "I have surely seen the oppression of My people who are in Egypt, and have heard their cry because of their taskmasters, for I know their sorrows" (Ex 3:7).

Praise God! It is so good to know that our God doesn't slumber nor sleep; He always watches over us. He is always mindful of us and aware of our situations. The people of God had been in that oppressed situation for a long time. Who knows? They may have been wondering, does God care? Is He aware of our situation? We often spend a great amount of our time pondering these questions instead of calling on Him for deliverance. It could be that as you read this word, you are facing a particular situation and you are wondering, will it ever be over? But one thing we should constantly bear in mind is that no storm lasts forever.

The word of God tells us in Jeremiah 33:3, "Call to Me, and I will answer you, and show you great and mighty things, which you do not know." So stop wondering about the situation, the "how and when;" just do as God commanded us to do in the time of our difficulties. The hard time you may be facing at the moment is your Egypt, but God has a promised land for you, a land that you do not know about. So call upon Him, and He will show it to you. Remember, it was only when the Israelites called out to God that He answered and delivered them.

Let's Pray

I pray that God will lift you up above your situations and circumstances. But you will have to call upon Him so He can show you His power. Be blessed and go forth in this faith.

CAST YOUR BURDEN UPON HIM

*Come to Me, all you who labor and are heavy
laden, and I will give you rest (Mt 11:28).*

The Lord invites us to come to Him and He will give
us rest. He wants us to cast our burdens on Him.
Unfortunately, many have come to Him but have yet to
experience this rest simply because they have not cast their
burdens upon Him as He invites us to do. It is for this very
reason that we find many Christians loaded down with all
kinds of problems—financial, family, sentimental, and many
more. When we do not accept the Lord's invitation, it results
in our being robbed of the joy and peace received when we
come to Jesus.

To better explain this, let me recount the experience of
a certain man who lived long ago in a remote countryside.
In those days, cars were a very rare and precious commodity,

and they were seldom seen in that area. One day, this man was returning home from a very long journey. As he traveled the road carrying a big and heavy load on his head, a pickup truck came by and the driver offered him a ride, assuring him rest from the heavy load he was carrying. He gladly accepted and sat in the back of the truck. However, despite the fact that he was assured rest from the load, the man kept the heavy bag on his head throughout the entire journey. He barely enjoyed the ride.

We may find this funny and say he was a crazy man, but there are many believers whose actions are no different from his. They have come to Jesus, but sad to say, they are still carrying the burdens of life upon their shoulders, no matter how much the voice of the Lord tells them to cast their burden upon Him. In this story, that driver with the pickup truck represents our Lord Jesus Christ promising us rest. The man is the many believers who are still suffering under life's burdens because they have not fully accepted the Lord's promise.

We come to Jesus so we can receive rest from life's burdens. I urge you not to hold onto your burden but hand it over to the Lord instead. **Cast it all upon Him,** and in turn, He will give you rest and sustain you throughout life's journey.

Let's Pray

Dear Lord, thank You for Your promises to me.
You said, "Come to Me, you who are weary
and burdened and I will give you rest."
So I give You my burden and accept Your rest
for my weary soul. **Amen.**

DISCOURAGEMENT

Don't let discouragement keep you from praying, for it is through prayer and faith in God that you will overcome. Don't let the spirit of discouragement use friends, family, or even strangers to discourage you. Be like David when his brothers tried to discourage him. The Bible says, "Then David spoke to the men who stood by him, saying, 'What shall be done for the man who kills this Philistine and takes away the reproach from Israel? For who is this uncircumcised Philistine, that he should defy the armies of the living God?' And the people answered him in this manner, saying, 'So shall it be done for the man who kills him.' Now Eliab his oldest brother heard when he spoke to the men; and Eliab's anger was aroused against David, and he said, 'Why did you come down here? And with whom have you left those few sheep in the wilderness? I know your pride and insolence of your heart, for you have come down to see the battle." And David said, 'What have I done now? Is there not a cause?'" (1 Sam 17:26-29).

David walked away from those who tried to discourage him. Sometimes the people who the enemy uses to discourage us can be very persistent. They are constantly on our back. But at times like these, we need to be like David – rebuke them and walk away. Never get down or lose focus. Whenever discouraging situations seem to linger, just use them as opportunities to go further just as Paul did:

> *But I want you to know, brethren, that the things which happened to me have actually turned out for the furtherance of the gospel, so that it has become evident to the whole palace guard, and to all the rest, that my chains are in Christ; and most of the brethren in the Lord, having become confident by my chains, are much more bold to speak the word without fear (Phil 1:12-14).*

It is not that bad things will never happen, but what matters is what you do in the midst of those bad circumstances.

Paul turned that bad situation into a good one. He reached out to the Roman soldiers who were part of the palace guard. He also used his experience to encourage those

Christians who were afraid of the persecution that was so prevalent at that time.

While our situations or circumstances might be different from Paul's prison experience, there are still plenty of opportunities that come our way with only one aim, and that is to discourage us. They may come in the form of financial challenges, family conflicts, etc. In the midst of his difficult situation, Paul looked for ways to stay faithful to God. Like Paul, finding out ways to remain faithful to God in the midst of difficult situations will in turn make our faith grow and our relationship with God become stronger.

Let's Pray

Dear Lord, help me to be mindful of Your presence in my life when situations or circumstances try to make me feel otherwise.
In Jesus' name, **Amen**.

DISTRACTION

Distraction is the diverting of the attention of an individual or group from the chosen object of attention onto the source of distraction. To divert means to turn aside from a specific path or cause. There are many people who have suffered "shipwrecks" in life because a spirit of distraction used various situations and circumstances to rob them of their focus.

The Bible gives us many examples of people who started out well but didn't finish well, because along the way the "distracter" came and diverted their attention from their goal. Ultimately, they were stopped from completing their journey. Some examples are people such as Adam and Eve, Lot's wife, Solomon, Judas the betrayer, and many other kings and prophets alike. We must understand that God's reward is not for those who just start the journey. Rather, it is for those who finish it. Matthew 24:13 tells us, "But he who endures to the end shall be saved."

When God liberated the children of Israel from Egypt, His intention was to take them to a vast land flowing with "milk and honey." However, out of the millions who left Egypt, only two and their descendants were able to step into that vast and good land. This happened because along the way, the children of Israel were distracted by the enemy. Satan knew God had a great plan for His people then and He still does today. Satan tried in every way to destroy them in Egypt, but he was unsuccessful. When they left Egypt, he was even more determined to stop them. He used whatever he could put his hands on—people, hunger, thirst, lust, fears, doubts. His efforts paid off, and he managed to stop a whole nation except for Joshua and Caleb.

Whenever the children of Israel encountered any situation, instead of trusting God for deliverance, they grumbled, murmured and complained. This is what the Lord had to say regarding their attitude when he spoke to Moses and Aaron:

> *How long shall I bear with this evil congregation who complain against Me? I have heard the complaints which the children of Israel make against Me. Say to them, As I live, says the Lord, just as you have spoken in My hearing, so I will do to you: The carcasses of you who have complained against Me shall fall in this wilderness, all of you were numbered according to your entire number, from twenty years old and above.*

Except for Caleb the son of Jephunneh and Joshua the son of Nun, you shall by no means enter the land which I swore I would make you dwell in. But your little ones, whom you said would be victims, I will bring in, and they shall know the land which you have despised. But as for you, your carcasses shall fall in this wilderness. And your sons shall be shepherds in the wilderness forty years and bear the brunt of your infidelity, until your carcasses are consumed in the wilderness (Num 14:27-33).

It is very common to find scriptures in the Bible where God warns His people to look ahead and turn neither to the left nor to the right. I believe that God is simply saying, "Let nothing distract you lest you fail to reach your destination." The word of God urges us to "Be sober, be vigilant; because your adversary the devil walks about like a roaring lion seeking whom he may devour" (1 Pt 5:8). Being vigilant is being watchful and not distracted. We are again told to look "...unto Jesus, the Author and Finisher of our faith" (Heb 12:2). So let us fix our eyes on Jesus and pray to Him to keep us focused on our journey, in Jesus' name.

Let's Pray

Thank You, Father, for Your strength that's perfect in my weakness. Help me to keep my eyes on You, Lord, especially when the lightning of life starts to flash and the thunder of trials starts to roll.

In Jesus' name I pray, **Amen**.

Don't Give up... Your Blessing is Coming

So the same day Pharaoh commanded the taskmasters of the people and their officers, saying, "You shall no longer give the people straw to make brick as before. Let them go and gather straw for themselves. And you shall lay on them the quota of bricks which they made before. You shall not reduce it"
(Ex 5:6-8).

At some point in our life, we all have faced certain situations that we thought were getting better but only became worse. This tends to happen because whenever the devil sees that we are about to receive our breakthrough, he works diligently to add on more troubles and pain to make the situation look more difficult or totally impossible. His aim is to create distractions and eventually destroy our hope, so he can rob us of our desire for freedom.

Pharaoh started to increase the labor of the Israelites only after Moses arrived in Egypt with the news of God's deliverance for them. Not only did he increase their workload, but he had them severely beaten by the taskmasters when they failed to produce the amount of work expected of them. Who was behind all this? The devil, of course. His aim and objective was to stop the people from obtaining their freedom. He did all that in an effort to turn their minds against Moses so they would not heed his words. He wanted the people to believe that Moses was the reason their situation had gotten worse. The devil hates to see people living in freedom, so he fights fiercely for them to lose hope and remain in bondage.

But friends, we all know that the delivery pain increases when a woman is about to give birth. This means that the closer she gets to bringing forth her baby, the more the pain intensifies and becomes unbearable. But it is at this point that she needs to push the hardest so she can give birth and end the pain.

So child of God, if you feel that your trouble is being increased, it is quite possible that you are on the verge of your breakthrough. So instead of focusing on the pain, think about what you are about to birth. Think about what you will receive and know that it will give you so much joy that you will totally forget the intensity of the pain you just experienced. **In light of this, my word to you is, Don't give up, but push harder. Your blessing is coming!**

Let's Pray

May the Lord grant you grace today to overcome whatever pain you are facing at this present time and to continue trusting Him for your victory, in Jesus' name, **Amen**.

EMPOWERED TO CONQUER

Blessed be the God and Father of our Lord Jesus Christ, who has blessed us with every spiritual blessing in the heavenly places in Christ (Eph 1:3).

I n his letter to the church in Ephesus, Paul asserts to the believers that their relationship with Christ has made them beneficiaries of every spiritual blessing that comes from heavenly places.

I believe it is God's will that every believer receive this great revelation. It is only then that we will take our rightful place in Christ and live in victory. Unfortunately, there are many Christians who live their lives feeling incomplete and powerless. They are practically bankrupt as beggars, simply because they have yet to receive this revelation into their hearts. In their opinion, there is still work to be done on God's part. However, this is contrary to God's word. According to verse 3, Paul is praising God for what has already been done—it is finished! Therefore, the problem rests on our side. Now it is up to us to receive the revelation of what has been accomplished for us and bestowed upon us through our union with Christ.

Once there was a man who decided to travel to another country. He purchased his ticket but did not take the time to learn what he was entitled to with that ticket. So in his ignorance, he assumed the worst and went ahead and bought enough crackers and cheese to sustain him on his journey; then he boarded the ship.

Throughout the course of his journey every morning, afternoon, and evening, he would look with longing as the other passengers made their way to the dining room to partake in the abundance of available food. Though there was more than enough for all to eat, this "poor and ignorant" passenger fed himself on his crackers and cheese. All the while he was desiring very much the opportunity to partake of the delicacies available in the dining room. His lack of participation did not go unnoticed. The ship's captain noticed that this man separated himself from everyone and was on the lookout for him as he disembarked when they reached their destination. The captain thought that without knowing, he or one of his crew members must have offended this passenger. So he called the man aside and began apologizing for whatever they had done that had caused him to refuse their hospitality. The captain explained that he never saw the man join in for breakfast, lunch or dinner during the entire trip. The "unfortunate" passenger quickly replied, "Certainly not! No one offended me. I chose not to participate because I perceived that it must be very costly for such high quality food and I could never afford it." In total astonishment, the captain replied, "But sir, the ticket you purchased was all-inclusive. The meals were part of the package!"

This story helps us to understand the mind-set of many believers who are starving themselves on their way to heaven although everything has been supplied for them. The Bible says, "He has blessed us," not "He will bless us." It is already included in the price He paid for us on Calvary. It's an all-inclusive-package. In his prayer, Paul expresses his desire for us to know and understand: "And what is the exceeding greatness of His power toward us who believe, according to the working of His mighty power" (Eph 1:19). Paul wanted us to realize the kind of power that is at our disposal. It is the same power that raised Christ from the dead and loosed Him from the pangs of death that has been made available to all of us believers.

My dear friend, if you received this revelation in your heart, you will triumph over every obstacle of the enemy in your life. For those who walk in this power, there is no unsolvable problem nor any impossibility. For we have been blessed with every spiritual blessing in the heavenly places. No wonder the scripture says, "I can do all things through Christ who strengthens me" (Phil 4:13). It's up to us to receive the revelation and walk in victory.

Let's Pray

Lord, help me to never forget Your provision for my journey, in Jesus' name I pray, **Amen.**

HERE I AM, LORD

Come now, therefore, and I will send you to Pharaoh that you may bring My people, the children of Israel, out of Egypt (Ex 3:10).

When God wanted to set the children of Israel free from slavery and the grip of Pharaoh, He needed to use a person. So he found Moses, and used him as an instrument to operate through to deliver the people. There are many instances in the Bible which prove to me that these people were family to Moses. His family needed someone who was courageous, willing and able to believe God to go up against the wicked Pharaoh and his system. He had to face Pharaoh and declare, "Thus says the Lord, 'Let My people go'!"

Without a doubt, this was not an easy task. It was indeed a great responsibility, and very risky, too. But Moses was willing to pay the price. The Lord Almighty is always looking for people like Moses who are willing to say, "Lord, here I am; send me." Just as the children of Israel were in physical bondage then, there are many people today who are in spiritual bondage. They are being held captive by Pharaoh (Satan) through all kinds of destructive habits, sicknesses, diseases, emotional and mental bondage. Many of these people are our own family members. We must open our ears and hear the cry of God saying, "Will you come now and let Me use you to stand in the gap for your home, your children, your brothers and sisters, parents, spouse?" In order for God to bring about the change He desires, He needs to find someone like Moses who is willing to go against the odds.

Throughout the Bible, we find people who cooperated with God as He brought about change. People like Noah, who worked tirelessly on building the ark and believed the promises of God in the midst of a crooked generation. That ark was later used for the deliverance of his family. We heard Joshua as he stood on the Word of God declaring that he and his house would serve the Lord. With this declaration, I see a man who was determined to face hell itself so that the Will of God for his family could prevail.

We see men like Jepthah. Even after being sent away from his father's house, he later returned to fight for them so that they would be safe. There are women like the Shunammite woman who defied death itself as she fought for the life of her son. I could go on and talk about Nehemiah, Esther, David,

Job, the Canaanite woman, Jairus, the Philippian jailer, all the way down to the church in the Book of Acts that prayed fervently for Peter's deliverance.

I have mentioned these people in the hope that we will also wake up to hear God's cry as He seeks to bring about changes in our own families. It is time to stand up and say, "God, I am ready to be a vessel in your hand to be used for The deliverance of my family." Therefore, "...believe in the Lord Jesus Christ, and you will be saved, you and your household" (Acts 16:31).

Let's Pray

Dear Lord, I pray that my ears will always be inclined to hear Your calling and my heart ready to follow Your instructions, in Jesus' name, **Amen.**

HEZEKIAH SOUGHT THE LORD

God! Our Refuge & Strength

O Lord of hosts, God of Israel, the One who dwells between the cherubim, You are God, You alone, of all the kingdoms of the earth. You have made heaven and earth. Incline Your ear, O Lord, and hear; open Your eyes, O Lord, and see; and hear all the words of Sennacherib, which he has sent to reproach the living God. Truly, Lord, the kings of Assyria have laid waste all the nations and their lands, and have cast their gods into the fire; for they were not gods, but the work of men's hands—wood and stone. Therefore they destroyed them. Now therefore, O Lord our God, save us from his

***hand, that all the kingdoms of the earth
may know that You are the Lord, You alone
(Is 37:16-20).***

When king Hezekiah said this prayer, he was facing a very difficult and disturbing situation, but it did not cause him to forget God. Instead, he sought the help of the Almighty God. Often, it is in difficult times like these that we show God how much we are depending on Him. Many people run to friends and family seeking refuge and protection in times of their difficulties because God seems very distant to them.

A common question that pops into their mind at such times is, "If God is with me, why all this?" What they really mean is, "If He couldn't stop that from happening, what guarantee do I have that He will deliver me from this?" I believe that it is because of thoughts like these that many people seek help from sources other than God. But how wrong they are. The truth is that God has never promised that the enemy would not come against us. But He did promise us that He will deliver us in times of trouble if we put our confidence in Him and call upon Him. His word tells us, "Call upon Me in the day of trouble; I will deliver you, and you shall glorify Me" (Ps 50:15), and "God is our refuge and strength, a very present help in trouble" (Ps 46:1).

"Many are the afflictions of the righteous, but the Lord delivers him out of them all" (Ps 34:19). God has promised us deliverance in times of our troubles. As believers, we must always be mindful of His promises to us. Then when the enemy comes against us, we don't lose our focus but take a stand against him just like Hezekiah did. Hezekiah knew trouble was against him, but he also knew who was above all of his troubles. So without fear, he received the letter announcing the trouble and ran to God with it and called upon Him for deliverance.

Praise God, for He always honors the faith of His people. Now let us look at the outcome of Hezekiah's trust in God:

> *Then Isaiah the son of Amoz sent to Hezekiah, saying, Thus says the Lord God of Israel, Because you have prayed to Me against Sennacherib king of Assyria, this is the word which the Lord has spoken concerning him: The virgin, the daughter of Zion, has despised you, laughed you to scorn; the daughter of Jerusalem has shaken her head behind your back!...Because your rage against Me and your tumult have come up to My ears, therefore I will put My hook in your nose and My bridle*

in your lips, and I will turn you back by the
way which you came (Is 37:21-22, 29).

The good thing about putting our trust and confidence in God and giving Him control of our lives is that our trouble becomes His trouble. Then, when the enemy comes against us, he is actually coming against God. So as a result of the enemy coming against king Hezekiah, God sent His angel to destroy the soldiers of Sennacherib. In despair, he returned to his home to worship his god who couldn't deliver him even while he was worshipping him. The Bible tells us that his own sons came and killed him, "Now it came to pass, as he was worshiping in the house of Nisroch his god, that his sons Adrammelech and Sharezer struck him down with the sword" (Is 37:38).

Let's Pray

Father, please help me to rest assured in Your promises and plan for my life. Help me to know that You are ever present in times of trouble, in Jesus' name I pray, **Amen.**

How is Your Love For Discipline?

What is discipline? Webster's dictionary defines it as "systematic training or subjection to authority." This occurs especially in the training of mental, moral, and physical powers by instruction and exercise.

Discipline is, therefore, sticking to a specific course of action as instructed in order to result in a habit of obedience that is subjection. The negative aspect of discipline is that it is never a pleasant experience. Discipline often causes discomfort; as human beings, we don't like to subject ourselves to discomfort. Above all, it requires us to be humble.

Lack of humility can cause the process of disciplining to become even more painful. Many people become very angry when being disciplined and resist the training process in whatever way possible. They refuse to subject themselves to instructions. Therefore, quite often the process of being disciplined is stopped and the training is incomplete.

Displaying a negative attitude toward discipline is common practice. This only results in us never attaining the level we are supposed to reach. It is very important that we come to terms with the fact that though discipline never comes to us in the way we want, it is always for our own good. Therefore, the training we receive today will only make us better tomorrow. As the Bible clearly puts it, "Only those who love knowledge love discipline." This means that the more we accept being disciplined—allowing ourselves to go through the systematic training process—the greater our knowledge will be.

Let me again point out the main reason why we resist discipline; it is simply because it comes with reproof. There is a show of disapproval to one's action, and we, who always think we are right, never like that. That is why it is important that we are humble. But the choice is ours! We can either accept correction and increase in knowledge, or resist/avoid it and remain stupid. These are not my words but God's: "Whoever loves instruction loves knowledge, but he who hates correction is stupid" (Prv 12:1).

Let's Pray

Lord my God, I pray that You give me a humble heart so that I can accept Your corrections, instructions and discipline in order to be a better believer and servant, in Jesus' name, **Amen**.

HOW REAL IS
YOUR WEALTH?

Let us take a moment and ask ourselves this question: "In what areas am I rich?" I don't know what your answer is. However, the fact of the matter is there are many people who are rich in worldly goods and some who are infamously rich in pride, annoyance, stubbornness, selfishness, etc. These are just a few examples of the many factors that cause people to miss the chance to acquire the real wealth—the precious pearl that makes one really rich. Missing this great opportunity places one in the same category the Lord Jesus was speaking about when He made reference to the spiritual condition of the church of the Laodiceans, "Because you say 'I am rich, have become wealthy, and have need of nothing' and do not know that you are wretched, miserable, poor, blind and naked" (Rev 3:17). How true this is, because what the world refers to as "being wealthy" is really not wealth in the sight of God.

The sad truth about the church of the Laodiceans is that during the time of their humble beginning, they knew true wealth. However, over the passage of time, their humbleness became worn out by the journey. Eventually, they began to think that because they had acquired a significant amount of material possessions, they were rich. Sad to say, it is in this same unfortunate situation that many believers find themselves today. They think that being wealthy is the actual accumulation of material goods. They have a misconception that they are wealthy, but they are in fact extremely poor in the sight of God. No one is exempt from this. If you have not been careful, it is possible that you may be one of them. I say to you, "Stop pretending to be rich and humble yourself under the mighty hand of God." Say to Him, "I acknowledge that what I have really doesn't make me rich because I am indeed poor. HELP ME!"

If you are willing to do this, you are seconds away from acquiring real wealth. Jesus will then enter and remain in the center of your life and make you rich. He is the Precious Pearl and those who possess Him, possess the true wealth.

Let's Pray

Father, I am a wretched sinner. Forgive me for the times that I pretended to be rich when truly in Your sight I am poor. Come into my life and stay in the center of it. I renounce all my pride and selfish attitude. I say come in and have Your way in my life. Help me not to ever go back to where You have rescued me from, in Jesus' name I pray, **Amen**.

Ignoring God's Mercy?

Woe to you, Chorazin! Woe to you, Bethsaida!
For if the mighty works which were done in
you had been done in Tyre and Sidon, they
would have repented long ago in sackcloth
and ashes. But I say to you, it will be more tol-
erable for Tyre and Sidon in the day of judg-
ment than for you. And you, Capernaum,
who are exalted to heaven, will be brought
down to Hades; for if the mighty works which
were done in you had been done in Sodom, it
would have remained until this day. But I say
to you that it shall be more tolerable for the
land of Sodom in the day of judgment that
for you (Mt 11:21-24).

Really, how much do we need to see before we are convinced that Jesus is Lord? These verses show

Jesus rebuking the cities where He did most of His miracles because of their unrepentant attitude. The people refused to change their way of living and surrender their lives to Him. This same rebuke can be applied to many people today. Even after seeing so many signs and wonders and receiving so many favors from the Lord, their hearts still remain hardened towards God.

We must not take the mercy of God for granted. Every time He operates in our life, we must see it not only as a blessing, but also as a warning. Remember, the same blessing we receive from God can be a witness against us in the day of judgment. The truth is that if the mercy of God that is shown to so many people today was shown to those who went before us without salvation, they would surrender their life to the Lord Jesus Christ and receive their salvation.

In spite of all these mighty miracles and great show of God's mercy toward them, many of these same individuals still act as though they have an eternity ahead of them to live. Instead of repenting and surrendering their life to the Lord, they continue to ignore the mercy of God and persist in their own way. But as it was in the days of Noah, so it will be in the end of time. Fellow believers, let's be wise and learn to see the mercy of God in our daily lives. Instead of casting it aside, let us use it as a stepping stone to get close to Him.

Let's Pray

Lord, help me not to take Your daily mercies in my life for granted, in Jesus' name, **Amen.**

IS YOUR FAITH BEING TESTED?

Throughout our lifetime on Earth, we need to always be willing to exercise our faith. The Bible advises us that if we desire to please our God, we must use our faith. It is written, "But without faith, it is impossible to please Him, for he who comes to God must believe that He is, and that He is a rewarder of those who diligently seek Him" (Heb 11:6). There are times when God will test our faith with the things that are dear to us just to see how much we trust in Him. So we should never allow fear to prevent us from letting go of anything in our care or possession. Releasing is one way we express our faith in God.

Just consider how much Moses was loved by his mother. But with her faith in God, she determined in her heart to let him go. By doing that, God's plan was fulfilled in his life. Suppose she had refused to do what she did. Her action would have prevented God's plan from being fulfilled in Moses' life and eventually would have brought disaster upon both of them. In addition, the suffering of God's people would have been prolonged. But by using her faith and taking that risk to let Moses go, she in turn pleased God. Thus the door of their future success and well-being was opened.

We must understand that all of this didn't happen just because she gave Moses up. First, she had to release herself from every fear. Then she had to release her faith and belief in God in order for things to work out for her good just as God promised in His word, "And we know that all things work together for good to those who love God" (Rom 8:28). Can you imagine what could have happened if she had allowed herself to be overcome with the fear of losing her baby boy and had continued hiding him? The possibilities are just endless.

Now my question to you is, "What is it in your life, at this moment in time, that God has been using to test your faith but you are afraid to release?" Remember, if Moses' mother had been afraid, she would not have seen God's glory in his or her life. So my prayer is that God will strengthen you to use your faith so that you will trust Him enough to take Him at His word and do what He is requiring of you. God Bless you.

Let's Pray

My God, please give me the courage to trust and obey Your instructions for my life even when it causes discomfort. Help me to be mindful of Your promise that everything works for the good of those who love You, **Amen**.

IT IS POSSIBLE!

Then Mary said to the angel, "How can this be, since I do not know a man?" And the angel answered and said to her, "The Holy Spirit will come upon you, and the power of the Highest will overshadow you" (Lk 1:34-35).

Mary questioned the possibility of conceiving a child since she had never known a man. In her eyes, she was totally incapable of meeting the requirements set before her. But knowing that nothing is impossible for God, the angel clearly explained to her that it was possible through the Holy Spirit and the power from on high.

Even though we are surrounded by many examples of God making the impossible possible, like Mary, many of us today question the possibility of doing what God is asking or requiring of us. We have the tendency to look at our ability and the "would be" obstacles. In our eyes, we are seemingly incapable; so we think God is mistaken. But learn this much, child of God: God is God and He knows all things. Before He speaks to us, He has already assessed the situation and knows exactly whether or not we are able to manage. In other words, I am saying that God knows our full capabilities and limitations. This is why He would never assign us something we are unable to do. So whenever He asks us to pursue a particular course of action, it is because He is quite certain of our ability to perform and complete it.

This is why we should not jump to the conclusion that just because we see something as impossible for us in our eyes, it is not impossible for God. In other words, just because we think we are unable to do something doesn't mean that we are right. When the opportunity was first presented to Mary, she quickly thought it was impossible—especially since she had never been with a man. But the Lord assured her that the mission she was to accomplish was possible, and she was humble enough to accept and believe.

So just as the Holy Spirit was there to help Mary produce what God wanted her to produce, He is still alive today and willing to help us accomplish what He wants us to. However, we must be willing to humble ourselves before God just as Mary did saying, Lord, Your will be done in my life, and I believe that with You all things are possible. So let us trust in God with all our heart and lean not on our own understanding. Amen.

Let's Pray

Father, often my own understanding tends to make me feel incapable of fulfilling my purpose. Lord Jesus, please help me to always look up to You and not lean on my own understanding, I pray, **Amen.**

KEEP YOUR PROMISE!

And the Lord spoke to Moses, 'Go to Pharaoh and say to him, "Thus says the Lord: Let My people go, that they may serve Me. But if you refuse to let them go, behold, I will smite all your territory with frogs"' (Ex 8: 1-2).

Because Pharaoh had refused to let the people go, God sent Moses to give him His message. He then commanded His servant to stretch out his hand with the rod over the streams, rivers and ponds; then frogs came and filled the land of Egypt. The Bible also tells us that this happened because Pharaoh hardened his heart and did not listen to the man of God.

Verses 6-7 tell us that the land was severely afflicted by this plague. When Pharaoh felt the pain and the trouble, verse 8 says that he called for Moses and Aaron and said to them, "Entreat the Lord that He may take away the frogs from me and from my people; and I will let the people go, that they may sacrifice to the Lord." But verse 15 says, "But when Pharaoh saw that there was relief, he hardened his heart and did not heed them." So when Pharaoh saw that there was relief, the Bible says he changed his mind and did not keep his promise to let the people go.

Like Pharaoh, during their times of trouble, pain, difficulty and affliction, many people make promises to God in the hope of finding relief. But as soon as the storm is over and they are no longer in pain, they feel relief and change their minds. They act as if they no longer remember their promises to God. Throughout my years of ministry and serving the Lord, I've had opportunities to minister to countless people who made many promises during their time of difficulty—promises like:

"When I get better, I will do this and that for the Lord. I'll change. I'll be a better person when God takes me out of this trouble. I will no longer get involved with things that will cause me to return to this situation." It goes on and on.

But as soon as the storm is over, the same spirit of unfaithfulness that was in Pharaoh gets into them. They harden their hearts and change their minds. They no longer desire to fulfill their promises to the Lord.

Friend, it is written in Ecclesiastes 5:4, "When you make a vow to God, do not delay to pay it; for He has no pleasure in fools. Pay what you have vowed." Keep your promise! "Better not to vow than to vow and not pay" (v. 5). Pharaoh thought he was being smart by not fulfilling his promise. But as seen in the word of God, he was being a fool. His action only opened the door for another, even bigger and more severe plague to come upon him and his people.

Let's Pray

God give us a faithful heart so that we can be
sincere with You, keep up with our promises,
and not be fools in Your sight
like Pharaoh was, **Amen**.

ONLY BE STRONG AND VERY COURAGEOUS!

Moses My servant is dead. Now therefore, arise, go over this Jordan, you and all this people, to the land which I am giving to them–the children of Israel, every place that the sole of your foot will tread upon I have given you, as I said to Moses (Jo 1:2-3).

After leading the people through the wilderness for forty years, Moses died. Then God called Joshua and told him to get ready to lead the people into the long-awaited promised land. Let's keep in mind that because of unbelief and rebellion against God, the older generation that left Egypt had all died, except for Joshua and Caleb. We see Joshua, who had been Moses' aide for forty years, receiving this great responsibility from God to lead over two million people into this new land. Above all, the Lord gave him the assurance of victory in verses 2 and 3. The basic principles of this victory are expressed in verse 7: "Only be strong and very courageous, that you may observe to do according to all the law which Moses My servant commanded you; do not turn from it to the right hand or to the left, that you may prosper wherever you go." Here we see God emphasizing the importance of Joshua reflecting a particular character, because this would be the key factor to his victory.

When God gave Joshua the promise, he could have very easily relaxed in his faith and let his guard down. But God knew that if Joshua did that, it would only result in failure. So to prevent that, He commanded Joshua to be strong—not physically but spiritually, so he could obey the voice of God without difficulty. Receiving the promise from God did not exempt Joshua from challenges. It is the same for us; we should know that we are not exempted either.

When challenges come, we must know that it is the enemy at work trying to discourage us so that we will lose heart, doubt God and eventually give up. When we read in the Bible about Joshua's mission, we definitely see that many hard times came his way with one aim: to stop him from doing what God had appointed him to do. But I'm sure that in Joshua's times of difficulty, He could clearly hear the voice of God in his heart loudly saying, "Only be strong and very courageous."

So dear friend, if you know God is with you and you have totally given your life to Him, just stay strong and keep running the race. Don't let trials get you down. The God of Joshua is your God. Remember, He told Joshua in verse 3 that for him to receive the land, he first had to touch it. You must bear in mind that the enemy doesn't want you to accomplish this because he knows that once you "touch," he has to lose it. For this reason, he works very hard to get you to lose your focus. But don't give him that pleasure! Fix your eyes on Jesus, for victory is assured in His name. Alleluia!

Let's Pray

Dear Lord, sustain me daily as I seek to
do Your will and fulfill my purpose,
in Jesus' name, **Amen**.

PEACE PERFECT PEACE

In every step of life, we find people who are constantly searching for things or activities to give them peace. Quite often in their search for peace, they get involved in situations that only add to their torment. Throughout my years of ministry, I believe the majority of people I have counseled fall into the category of those searching for peace and fulfillment in life. The fact is that many have died without acquiring this peace. It is sad to see the countless others who are continuing on the same path hoping that they will achieve peace. The Bible clearly points us to the way to acquire this perfect peace in Isaiah 26:3, and that is by trusting in God and keeping our mind on Him.

To explain this "perfect peace," let us glance at the meaning of perfect. Webster's dictionary defines it as "having all the qualities, excellences, or elements that are requisite to its nature or kind." In simpler terms, *without defect or lack*. So this tells us that the perfect peace is the kind that has no defect nor lacks in anything. It is the peace that is so perfect that life's troubles cannot disturb it. This peace is incomparable. The peace that many tend to receive from things or activities is temporary and simply does not compare to the perfect peace.

I remember when, in my effort to acquire perfect peace, I used to drink myself to sleep believing that I would have the peace and tranquility that I longed for. But the truth is, not only was it "make-believe," but it was severely short-lived; it was all temporary. Because as soon as the effects of the alcohol left my system, I was back to square one. I was the same sad and empty person, oftentimes even worse than I had been before. But just as I was then, there are many people who continue to seek their peace from elements or activities such as drugs, smoking, sex, and more. Though they realize that the peace they receive from these things is only temporary, they keep going from one thing to the next hoping they will finally find what they are seeking.

The fact is that no matter where one looks, the result will always be wrong if it is from the wrong source. We must understand that not only are these sources temporary and deceiving, but they also greatly contribute to mankind's destruction.

The only way mankind is able to find perfect peace is by turning to God. The peace that comes from God is permanent and without lack or defect. It is also pure and clean in its entirety. One word sums it up: PERFECT. This perfect peace is free for all who need it. To acquire it, all you have to do is to trust in God 100 percent. You must keep your mind on Him and let Him lead you to the way of **"peace, perfect peace."**

Let's Pray

Dear Lord, help me to trust in You with all my heart and to keep my mind on You so that in this world of trials and troubles, I can have Your perfect peace,

Amen.

THE POISON OF THE GOSSIPERS

To get to the heart of this problem, let's start with the following: "You shall not go about as a talebearer among your people; nor shall you take a stand against the life of your neighbor: I am the Lord" (Lv 19:16). "If anyone among you thinks he is religious, and does not bridle his tongue but deceives his own heart, this one's religion is useless" (Jas 1:26). And finally, "But no man can tame the tongue. It is an unruly evil, full of deadly poison" (Jas 3:8).

People who give in to the sin of gossiping are like poisonous snakes; their heads are filled with all sorts of poison ready to spew and destroy the life, character, relationship, etc., of others. Many people have become victims of their own deception. The saying goes, "Prevention is better than cure." How true this is. Curing the damage of gossip can prove to be very difficult. The way to prevent this damage is to have discernment. Having discernment helps you to know a gossiper right away. By knowing them, you are able to detect when they are heading your way, which is key to preventing the damage of gossip in your life.

In spite of all this, it is still not always easy to see them coming, because the spirit that influences gossiping is very cunning. Gossipers will not let you know that they are about to involve you in gossiping. Oftentimes, they present themselves in friendly and subtle ways with pretty smiles. If they are in a religious setting, they will pretend to be very spiritual and they may even give gifts to their prey. All these are ways of gaining access into the heart of their prey. Only after they have gained sufficient ground do they start their destructive work.

Another tactic of the gossiper is to start to talk about someone as if they don't want to hurt that person but are concerned for his or her "well-being." However, if the victim (listener) doesn't have spiritual discernment to realize where the conversation is heading and quickly stop it, the gossiper's two-fold mission of defamation of someone's character and ultimate contamination of the listener with rumors and lies will eventually become complete. Here is what the scripture says about those who listen to gossipers: "An evildoer gives heed to false lips; a liar listens eagerly to a spiteful tongue" (Prv 17:4).

Here is a story that will give greater insights into the damaging effects of gossiping and spreading misinformation.

Once there was a preacher who loved souls so much that he would go anywhere to rescue them. One day, he met a man who was an alcoholic, and after much evangelism and prayer, the man accepted Christ. However, as a new believer, this man needed much attention and help as he fought to overcome his struggle with this destructive habit. Knowing this, the loving and caring preacher was there for him every step of the way. It happened that this new believer accepted an invitation to a wedding where his friends insisted that one drink would not hurt him. But one drink was all it took for him to succumb to his drinking habit.

The preacher, not giving up, would go to the bar each time to take the man from that negative environment. On one such occasion, as the preacher walked down the steps from the bar arm-in-arm with the man, he stumbled and fell to the bottom. At that very moment, a member of his congregation by the name of "Sister Gossiper" was passing by and saw when the preacher hit the bottom of the steps. Her first thought was, "Oh my God! Pastor had been drinking and is so drunk that he fell down the stairs."

Being very spiritual, as she thought herself to be, she became so enraged about the "preacher's sin" that she began phoning every church member saying, "Do you know what I just saw my pastor doing…?" The story spread so quickly and with such poison that it only took a few days before many members of the congregation began to exhibit a negative attitude toward the preacher. The preacher, being totally ignorant of the whole affair, noticed a changed attitude toward him from his congregation and began to inquire as to the reason for their rather sudden change. Unable to bear it any longer, one of the deacons said to him, "Brother, your sin has been found out!" Surprised, the preacher responded, "What sin?!" The deacon answered, "Don't deny the fact that you were drunk last week. Sister Gossiper saw you when you fell down the stairs of the local bar."

My question is, "What is so wrong about this story so far?" The answer is that Sister Gossiper had ignored some very basic biblical principles, one of them being to love her brother. By not loving her brother, she thought evil of him and defamed his character. She totally ignored the word of God which tells us that *love* "...does not behave rudely, does not seek its own, is not provoked, thinks no evil" (1 Cor 13:5).

People who gossip do not really care about others, especially those they are gossiping about. They just want to have juicy information to attract others to themselves. But God's word contradicts this practice and says, "Let each of you look out not only for his own interests, but also for the interests of others" (Phil 2:4). So as believers, we should know the danger of indulging in gossip and pray to be free from the spirit that influences such practices.

The apostle Paul said, "Let each of us please his neighbor for his good, leading to edification" (Rom 15:2). Therefore, as believers, we should only consider words that build others up and not tear them down. The Bible affirms this: "Let no corrupt word proceed out of your mouth, but what is good for necessary edification, that it may impart grace to the hearers" (Eph 4:29).

The Bible further tells us, "Moreover if your brother sins against you, go and tell him his fault between you and him alone. If he hears you, you have gained your brother" (Mt 18:15). This is another important principle that Sister Gossiper ignored.

To continue this story, once the preacher realized what had triggered these reactions from his members, he backtracked the gossip to Sister Gossiper. She shamefully admitted that she started everything. The loving preacher then explained the real story to her. He told her that he had gone into the bar to plead with the man who had fallen back in his walk with Christ and succumbed to alcohol. He said that he urged him to leave with him, and it was while they were going down the stairs that he stumbled and fell. That was what she saw. At this point, Sister Gossiper was feeling very bad about the whole situation and her part in starting the rumor. She quickly asked for forgiveness and promised to go back to those whom she had gossiped to and tell them the real story.

Of course the preacher forgave her, but not without teaching her a lesson on how damaging the poison of gossip can be. He took her, along with a feather pillow, up to the top of a very tall building. Once there, he cut open the pillow and released the feathers into the wind. As they watched the feathers floating throughout the town, he told Sister Gossiper, "Go and retrieve all the feathers and don't fail to bring back every single one of them." She replied in dismay that it was impossible for her to retrieve every feather. The pastor told her that she was absolutely right about that. He explained that the feathers were just like the gossip she released throughout the community. No matter how hard she tried, she would never be able to retrieve all the false accusations. Because of her gossiping, there would always be some doubt and negative thoughts floating around out there about him and his character. How sad it is that some people will only learn their lesson at the expense of another person's reputation.

Gossiping has been a very strong instrument in the hands of the enemy, and many families are being destroyed as a result of it. Friendships and other relationships, as well as many organizations, including churches, have severely suffered the consequences of this evil. As innocent and subtle as it may seem when it is presented, if gossip is not dealt with in a timely manner, it will cause great and often lasting and damaging effects to all involved.

Sometimes gossip can start based upon an actual fact that, because of the sensitivity of the information, should not have been discussed in the first place. After being passed around for a while, going from one mouth to the next, with each person giving his own version, the information gets distorted. The Bible clearly shows how the tongue, this small member of our body, can bring about great destruction. It says:

> *Even so the tongue is a little member and boasts great things. See how great a forest a little fire kindles! And the tongue is a fire, a world of iniquity. The tongue is so set among our members that it defiles the whole body, and sets on fire the course of nature; and it is set on fire by hell (Jas 3:5-6).*

The Bible further expresses the difficulty in bringing it under control: "But no man can tame the tongue. It is an unruly evil, full of deadly poison" (Jas 3:8). So, if you now find yourself caught in the trap of a gossiping spirit, repent and ask God to help you overcome this destructive habit that will eventually cost you a very high price if you don't stop it now.

On the other hand, if you have been listening to gossipers, read Proverbs 17:4 again, and the next time you are approached by gossipers bringing you the story of someone's life, do not entertain them. Just let them know that if they have something to say about another person, the best way to handle it is to go to the person in question and discuss it with him or her. Using this method will help the gossipers to think about their weakness.

Here are some very important instructions to always remember to keep you away from the poison of gossiping:

> *Keep your tongue from evil, and your lips from speaking deceit. Depart from evil and do good; seek peace and pursue it. The eyes of the Lord are on the righteous, and His ears are open to their cry (Ps 34: 13-15).*

Let's Pray

Dear Lord, may the words of my mouth and the meditation of my heart be acceptable in Your sight. Bless my mouth to speak truth and my ears to hear only what is positive.
In Jesus' name I pray, **Amen**.

RELEASE THE PRAISE!

Then Mary took a pound of very costly oil of spikenard, anointed the feet of Jesus, and wiped His feet with her hair. And the house was filled with the fragrance of the oil (Jn 12:3).

What Mary did for the Lord showed the condition of her heart toward Him. Mary knew that what the Lord had already done and would do for her in the future far exceeded her own act of love toward Him. This act showed her humility and servant's heart, because in those days, it was the responsibility of the servant to attend to the feet. When a believer finally acknowledges the Lord for who He is, his or her greatest desire is to serve and please Him. Another great desire of a faithful servant is to see the Master happy. Therefore, the servant doesn't measure the amount of sacrifice necessary to please the Master.

According to scripture, Mary's act of devotion was very costly, but she didn't care. All she wanted was to please her Lord. She knew that it was not about her; rather, it was all about the Master. Therefore, the fragrance of her service filled the room. By the beautiful fragrance of her service, everyone realized that she had paid a high price for it. Our service has a fragrance. It is very important for us to understand that its scent determines its quality. In other words, the quality of your service to the Master is rated by its fragrance. The Bible tells us that Judas was very disturbed by Mary's act of devotion to the Master. He inquired, "Why was this fragrant oil not sold for three hundred denarii and given to the poor?" (Jn 12:5). But this was just the enemy manifesting his resistance to Mary's service.

My dear friend, if what we do for the Lord does not bother the enemy, we really need to examine the quality of our service.

The enemy does not mind too much when we do things casually or carelessly for the Lord. But he is very much disturbed when he sees us putting forth our best for the Master. He is disturbed when he sees us performing our service for the Master with a clean and willing heart. Mary spent over one year's wages just to demonstrate her love, devotion and loyalty to the Master. The enemy knows acts like that move the hand of the Master to release His favor and His blessings upon our lives. His words tells us, "For the eyes of the Lord run to and fro throughout the whole earth, to show Himself strong on behalf of those whose heart is loyal to Him" (2 Chr 16:9).

We must release our best to Him if we want Him to release His best to us. So if you want God's best, you must give Him your best—the best of your service, the best of your time, the best of your wealth, and above all, release your best praise to Him. Let the fragrance of your service fill the atmosphere. Make the enemy uncomfortable; let him plug his ears; let him smash his head; let him scream; let him criticize; and so on. But also know that as a believer in God's presence, giving your best is the secret to your victory. Know that the Lord will defend you when you give your best just as He did for Mary when He said,

> *Let her alone. Why do you trouble her? She has done a good work for Me. For you have the poor with you always, and whenever you wish you may do them good; but Me you do not have always. She has done what she could, she has come beforehand to anoint My body for burial. Assuredly, I say to you, wherever this gospel is preached in the whole world, what*

this woman has done will also be told as a memorial to her (Mk 14:6-9).

Let's Pray

Dear Lord Jesus, help me to honor You daily with the best of all that You've blessed me with, I pray, **Amen.**

THE NOW RESURRECTION POWER

I am the Resurrection and the Life. He who believes in Me though he may die, he shall live (Jn 11:25).

Jesus declared Himself to be "the Resurrection and the Life." It is His desire to see this power taking effect in the life of all those who believe in Him. However, unbelief and lack of knowledge are keeping many believers from having this experience. They are just like Martha. While Jesus was referring to the "Now Resurrection," all she was considering was the resurrection of the "Last Day." This is where many believers find themselves in life; they are stuck in "when we all get to heaven." This is very nice and beautiful, but the God whom I will be serving in heaven is the same God I believe in now. So there is nothing He will do then that He cannot do now.

After walking her through the process of believing in the "Now Resurrection," Jesus arrived at the tomb of Lazarus. He commanded them to roll away the stone, which is symbolic of unbelief and doubts. Therefore, for the power of God to get inside our tomb, we must remove the stone of doubt and unbelief. We must believe that God is not only interested in the "Last Day" part of our life; He desires to be glorified in our life today. Somebody shout, Now Resurrection!

Jesus said in John 5:25, "Most assuredly, I say to you, the hour is coming, and now is, when the dead will hear the voice of the Son of God; and those who hear will live." I believe Lazarus was in church that day; and while he was in the grave, the only thing he was waiting to hear was the voice of the Son of God. When He heard His voice, he wasted no time.

He could hardly help himself because of how wrapped up he was; but in spite of that, he fought his way to the door. He didn't want to miss the opportunity to experience the Resurrection Power in his life. He said, "This is my day!"

For this to be your day, you must recognize that you have been in this situation long enough and need to become violent in your desire to be out of it. Lazarus exemplifies the word of God, which tells us in Matthew 11:12, "...the violent take it by force." Lazarus chose to be violent, and he defied death. Are Jesus' words coming against your condition? Are you willing to be violent against your grave? The choice is yours.

Are you willing to believe in the "NOW" Resurrection Power! If Lazarus defied death, you, too, can defy that sickness, that family problem, or any problem affecting your life. So hear Jesus calling you out of that grave. Declare that today is your day! As Jesus was then, so He is now.

You've got to be like Lazarus and be able to hear the voice of Jesus from the bottom of your grave. Remember that the violent take it by force.

In Adam, we were born into death and were born to die. In Christ, we have been reborn in life and resurrected to live, "For as in Adam all die, even so in Christ all shall be made alive" (1 Cor 15:22)

Matthew 27:52 shows the revolt of some saints. Even while Jesus was dying on the cross, they were claiming their rights and leaving the grave behind: "And the graves were opened; and many bodies of the saints who had fallen asleep were raised." Know that He has done it for others and He will do it for you.

Let's Pray

My God, in the name of Jesus, I pray
that You will help me to keep my eyes on You
at all times, and to know that You are the
same yesterday, today and forever, **Amen**.

Revolt Against Injustice!

Then the children of Israel did evil in the sight of the Lord. So the Lord delivered them into the hand of Midian for seven years, and the hand of Midian prevailed against Israel. Because of the Midianites, the children of Israel made for themselves the dens, the caves, and the strongholds, which are in the mountains. So it was, whenever Israel had sown, Midianites would come up; also Amalekites and the people of the East would come up against them. Then they would encamp against them and destroy the produce of the earth as far as Gaza, and leave no sustenance for Israel, neither sheep nor ox nor donkey. For they would come up with their livestock and their tents, coming in as numerous as locusts; both they and their camels were without number; and they would enter

> *the land to destroy it. So Israel was greatly*
> *impoverished because of the Midianites, and*
> *the children of Israel cried out to the Lord*
> *(Jgs 6:1-6).*

This was a period of distress, shame and humiliation for the people of God. They were severely afflicted by the hand of their enemies. One wrong decision had paved the way to the land of injustice. They not only had to work hard, but at the time of harvest, they also had to see their enemy come and take away what they had labored for so tirelessly.

They suffered for seven long years with this dilemma—working for their enemy. This was blatant injustice, so much so that their enemies left no sustenance for them. Finally, when Israel could do nothing to help get themselves out of the situation, they remembered the God of justice, the One who has no pleasure in injustice. The Lord heard their cry and sent a prophet to remind them of God's faithfulness to them saying,

> *I brought you up from Egypt and brought you*
> *out of the house of bondage; and I delivered you*
> *out of the hand of the Egyptians and out of the*
> *hand of all who oppressed you, and drove them*
> *out before you and gave you their land (Jgs*
> *6: 8-9).*

Now, was it God's desire to deliver them out of that terrible situation? Of course it was! But He needed to find someone who was not only a victim of injustice, but was also revolted against the situation and willing to fight for justice to prevail. There are many people who are victims of injustice, but a lack of revolt against it and unwillingness to fight for their justice has left them with continuous hardship and suffering. If you are not happy with your present situation, it is easy to hope for a change. But hope alone cannot bring about the changes you desire. You must revolt against the situation and be willing to pay the price for change.

The word of God tells us that faith without works is dead. So your hope for change must be accompanied by action. The people of God wanted change but at the same time were hiding in caves, in strongholds, and in mountains. But there must come a time when we get so revolted against the situation that we refuse to stay in the "caves" and say, "Come what may, happen what happens, I am going to fight for a better life. Enough of this injustice!"

So God found a man by the name of Gideon, a man who refused to stay in the cave. He was out threshing the wheat in a winepress in an effort to keep it from the Midianites. I am sure in his heart he was saying, "I am tired of this shame. I am tired of this abuse, this injustice! There must be something better than this." Are you tired of your situation?

In verse 12 we see, "And the Angel of the Lord appeared to him, and said to him, 'The Lord is with you, you mighty man of valor!'" These words proved that God was pleased with the attitude and faith of Gideon. He called him a mighty man of valor. Gideon couldn't accept that God was with him and at the same time live a life of defeat. He knew about His God. He knew God could do better than that. He knew that if God could deliver His people in the past, He could deliver them from the present situation. As He was then, He still operates the same way today.

The Bible says that our God changes not; Jesus Christ is the same, yesterday, today and forever. From everlasting to everlasting, He is God. God was attracted by Gideon's courage: "Then the Lord turned to him and said, 'Go in this might of yours, and you shall save Israel from the land of the Midianites. Have I not sent you?'" (Jgs 6:14)

God encouraged Gideon to keep going in that faith to save Israel out of their dilemma. For a moment, the calling to be a deliverer of God's people weighed heavily on Gideon. He began looking at his background and his capacity. This is what happens to many people when an opportunity for change comes. They began looking at their surroundings, family background, educational level, and more. But God wants us to know that it is not where we are coming from nor who and what is around us, but rather, the belief in our heart and God on our side. This is what will take us to the level God wants us to reach and eventually bring about the desired changes in our lives.

"And the Lord said to him. 'Surley I will be with you, and defeat the Midianites as one man'" (v. 16). I believe that like Gideon, we are all called to make a difference in this world. We must stop spending time making excuses and reminding God of our limitations as if He doesn't know all about us. Doing this implies that He has made a mistake in evaluating our character.

Let us remember that God has promised us the tools and strength we need to overcome.

> *Commit your way to the Lord, trust also in Him, and He shall bring it to pass. He shall bring forth your righteousness as the light, and your justice as the noonday (Ps 37:5-6).*

Let's Pray

Lord, please help me to be aware of the traps that the enemy uses to try to keep me in bondage. Help me to stand as Gideon did and overcome all that the enemy brings across my path, **Amen.**

The Avenue of Faith Leads to Victory!

And He said to them, 'Which of you shall have a friend, and go to him at midnight and say to him, Friend, lend me three loaves; for a friend of mine has come to me on his journey, and I have nothing to set before him;' and he will answer from within and say, 'Do not trouble me; the door is now shut, and my children are with me in bed; I cannot rise and give to you?' I say to you, though he will not rise and give him because he is his friend, yet because of his persistence he will rise and give to him as many as he needs (Lk 11:5-8).

The moral of this story is that persistence is key to victory. In this parable, the Lord directs us down a wonderful path that we can travel throughout life; it is the "Avenue of Faith." In this account given by the Lord Jesus, a person in need tries to acquire three loaves of bread from a friend. It appears obvious that his friend was his only hope. At first, the friend refused his request due to the hour of night and the inconvenience it would have caused him since he was already in bed.

So mere friendship was not enough to get the man what he needed; therefore, he was stuck. How many people are stuck in life because their ability, condition, educational level, immigration status, or other things have proven insufficient to qualify them for what they want to accomplish in life. For this reason, many people are giving up on their dreams and their hopes. The enemy has them caught up in their lack of physical, mental and material ability.

But based on what our Lord is teaching us in this passage, there is another avenue that we can use to overcome, and that is by faith.

Jesus said that friendship is not enough to make a friend get up and give you the three loaves; but by using faith, you will get even more than three loaves. "I say to you, though he will not rise and give to him because he is his friend, yet because of his persistence he will rise and give him as many as he needs" (Lk 11:8). That is what faith does; it makes you an overcomer. It makes you experience God's abundance. No wonder the Bible calls us to live by faith: "Now the just shall live by faith" (Heb 10:38). On the basis of friendship, he could only expect to get three loaves; but by faith, he could get as many as he wanted.

There are so many Christians, I mean "good Christians," who go to church faithfully and pray constantly; yet they live a life of mediocrity simply because they have refused to live by the faith principle. They keep leaning on their physical ability, and when this proves to be insufficient, they give up and let the enemy have the upper hand in their lives. Giving up is the sign that you are not living by faith. Because when you live by faith, you don't give up! You don't quit! Press on to the end, and you fight for what you believe.

If you know there are "loaves" to take care of your needs, you will persevere until you get them. You must understand that the devil doesn't want you to have victory in life. So whenever you decide to do something that will build up your life, he will always try to discourage you. He will present you with so many *no*s. But if you know the Avenue of Faith and keep walking on it, you know that his "no" will not impede you. Take Zacchaeus for example:

> *Then Jesus entered and passed through Jericho. Now behold, there was a man named Zacchaeus who was a chief tax collector, and he was rich. And he sought to see who Jesus was, but could not because of the crowd, for*

> *he was of short stature. So he ran ahead and*
> *climbed up into a sycamore tree to see Him, for*
> *He was going to pass that way (Lk 19:1-4).*

Zacchaeus's heart's desire was to see Jesus. But when he tried physically, he encountered a problem because he was short and the crowd was large. The Bible tells us that when he failed physically, he did not quit; he used his faith and ran ahead of the crowd. God showed him a tree, which he climbed. Praise God!

Whenever you take the Avenue of Faith, God will always show you a way out. Only minutes earlier, Zacchaeus was so low that he couldn't see Jesus. But after using his faith, he was up in the tree that allowed him to have the greatest view. His view was far better than that of anyone below on the ground. Why was this so? Because when he ran ahead, he used faith. You must learn to run ahead of the crowd of obstacles, doubts, fears, discouragements, and all the rest for God to make a better life for you.

All Zacchaeus wanted was to see Jesus, but because he used his faith, he got more than just a view of Jesus. He got the opportunity to have Jesus as his guest and to sit at the table with Him. He also got the opportunity to receive salvation for his household and to have his name written in the Holy Bible—God's book. But for all these things to happen for him, Zacchaeus had to take the faith avenue. Friend, do you know which avenue you are on? Remember, only the Avenue of Faith leads to victory.

May the Lord teach us to run ahead of the "crowd" in Jesus' name.

Let's Pray

Lord, I pray that you will always keep me on the Avenue of Faith, in Jesus' name, **Amen**.

THE BLESSINGS OF WAITING ON THE LORD

The Abram said, "Look, You have given me no offspring; indeed one born in my house is my heir!" And behold, This one shall not be came to him, saying, "This one shall not be your heir, but one who will come from your own body shall be your heir" (Gen 15: 3-4).

Abram had been walking with God for quite a number of years. Throughout that time, his willing obedience to God's instructions led him to acquire great wealth. However, there was one burden that he needed to be freed from, and that was the lack of children of his own. In a conversation with God, he lamented that the lack of an offspring would cause a stranger, born in his house, to be his heir. But God promised him that this would not be so. And the Bible says that he believed God.

Receiving and believing the promises of God until they are fulfilled comes with gaps of time of various lengths. I often refer to these gaps as the "process." This is the period of time we have to stand in faith and confidence in spite of the opposition that comes against us. Because quite often, it is during this time that our faith is tested, tried and proven. Know that the moment we believe the promise of God, we conceive. But if we allow the process to wear us out and begin doubting the God of the promise, we activate an abortion of the promise we initially conceived through our belief. Therefore, for us to have that promise fulfilled, we would have to start all over again.

After Abram received God's promise of an offspring, it appeared throughout the process as if that promise would never be fulfilled in his life. His wife, Sarai, began to focus more on her physical limitations than on God making the impossible possible. She manifested an impatient spirit that reinforced her doubt in God's promise to the point that she said to her husband, "See now, the Lord has restrained me from bearing children. Please, go in to my maid; perhaps I shall obtain children by her. And Abram heeded the voice of Sarai" (Gen 16:2).

The character Sarai manifested is no different from what many people manifest today. She became impatient after allowing the length of the process and the knowledge of her condition to wear her out. She began acting on her own strength to bring the fulfillment of the promise to pass. The words of the Psalmist David tell us clearly, "Unless the Lord builds the house, they labor in vain who build it" (Ps 127:1). In other words, anything we build without God being the Master Builder will never bring us any joy or satisfaction in life. We will still be empty and His promise unfulfilled in our lives. So all the work we do with our own strength, ideas, plans, and the like, will have been a waste—just laboring in vain.

The result of Sarai's action is a prime example of laboring in vain. All her effort to get the work done proved to be in vain. After all was said and done, she discovered that she only added to her sorrow:

> *Then Sarai said to Abram, "My wrong be upon! I gave my maid into your embrace; and when she saw that she had conceived, I became despised in her eyes. The Lord judge between you and me" (Gen 16:5).*

As a result of this action of doubt, Sarai had to live with the misery that resulted for many years. As for Abram, he did not hear anything from God for over thirteen years. Abram was ninety-nine when God appeared to him again.

I believe that the conceiving process had to be restarted. This time when God appeared to Abram, He cleared up any misconception that Abram had by saying, "I am Almighty God; walk before Me and be blameless" (Gen 17:1). In other words, "Trust Me; I am able to do all things." So in the process of time, as Abram obeyed God's last instruction to him, God's promise was fulfilled in his life.

The Bible says, "Now to Him who is able to do exceedingly abundantly above all that we ask or think, according to the power that works in us" (Eph 3:20). Just standing firm in our trust and confidence in God for a specific promise to be fulfilled can cause God to add to us what we never thought of or asked Him for. God promised Abram an offspring but took it a step further and promised to make him father of a nation. He changed their names to reflect how much He wanted this. Abram was renamed Abraham and Sarai became Sarah. This time, Abraham stood in his faith and believed God. So in due time, God visited Sarah and she conceived and brought forth a son, "And Sarah said, 'God has made me laugh, and all who hear will laugh with me'" (Gen 21:6).

Look how good our God is. When we trust and wait on Him, He will make us laugh. His word tell us, "The blessing of the Lord makes one rich, and He adds no sorrow with it" (Prv 10:22). But many times, what comes by our own efforts brings a lot of sorrow, just as the birth of the child by Sarai's maidservant caused Sarai much grief.

Dear friend, it is time we sit down and consider our ways and see if we are really trusting God or trying to make things happen by our own efforts. Because making things happen by our own efforts will only cause us sorrow. May the Lord deliver us in Jesus' name.

Dangers of a
Bitter Heart

Pursue peace with all people, and holiness, without which no one will see the Lord: looking carefully lest anyone fall short of the grace of God; lest any root of bitterness springing up cause trouble, and by this many become defiled (Heb 12:14-15).

At some point in our life, we have been or will be hurt. How we deal with our hurt can either stop bitterness from germinating in us or cause it. Whether the hurt was intentional or unintentional, if it is not dealt with immediately, it will become a seed of bitterness implanted deeply in our heart. Sometimes people may not mean to hurt us, but we are overly sensitive; the offense is really just in our imagination. No one has hurt us, but somehow we feel that the person's intention was to do just that. Of course, the perfect soil for bitterness to germinate and grow is a heart that harbors hostility and has not learned to deal with life's hurts in a godly manner.

Because we do not deal with our hurt in a godly manner, it results in bitterness taking root in our heart. Consequently, we live our lives always looking for faults in others, things to criticize and people to blame for our dilemma. In simple terms, we look for ways to justify the despair, desperation and depression we are feeling. But none of these practices will eradicate bitterness from our heart; in fact, they will only add to it. When people become bitter in life, they ultimately are restless and never at peace. They become proficient in knowing how to push others' "hot buttons." They aggravate others until they react in a way that gives them further justification for their bitterness. To affirm this attitude, they say, "I knew it; I was right. I do have reason to be bitter."

People filled with bitterness are very difficult to deal with. They are either looking for sympathy or trouble. The spirit that works through bitterness is a very tricky one. It knows how to hide and disguise itself. Because these people have not done what they were supposed to do, they hardly ever admit that they are bitter. They will either deny or disguise it. There is a tendency for a person filled with bitterness to be insincere or ungrateful, to have mood swings and to hold many grudges. Bitterness affects a person physically, spiritually and emotionally; it eats him or her up like cancer. If these words have helped you to identify a hurt that has caused you to have bitterness in your heart, here are some tips that will help you eradicate it from your life:

1. Don't be afraid to say you don't know your heart. Just ask God to reveal the condition of your heart to you. Only God knows your heart. It is written, "The heart is deceitful above all things, and desperately wicked; who can know it?" (Jer 17:9). So let the Holy Spirit do a radical scanning of your heart.

2. Ask God's forgiveness for being a bitter person and for keeping Him out of your life all this time. If someone hurts you, ask Him to give you the strength to forgive that person and move on.

3. Remember, just as God was merciful to you, you must be merciful to those who offend you. Seek peace at all times. It is written, "Pursue peace with all people, and holiness, without which no one will see the Lord" (Heb 12:14).

If you really want to see the Lord, you have to implement these things in your life. When you deal with your bitterness, you will discover the blessing of a healthy heart. You will be more happy and joyful as the word of God tells us, "A merry heart does good, like medicine, but a broken spirit dries the bones" (Prv 17:22).

The Dangers of Pride

How you are fallen from heaven, O Lucifer, son of the morning! How you are cut down to the ground, you who weakened the nations! For you have said in your heart: I will ascend into heaven, I will exalt my throne above the stars of God; I will also sit on the mount of the congregation on the farthest sides of the north; I will ascend above the heights of the clouds, I will be like the Most High (Is 14:12-14).

Pride is one of the most dangerous sins. Once rooted in a person's life, it will gradually work its way to eventually destroy the person. No one is immune to pride. Therefore, no one can say, "I don't have to worry because I've taken my antidote. I will not be pride's victim." We must understand that pride is a sin that every one of us must guard ourselves against on a daily basis. In order for us not to deceive ourselves, we must take this approach with a true and sincere heart.

The scripture above clearly proves to us that pride is the reason why Lucifer became Satan. The word Lucifer means "light bearer." How sad this is to go from light bearer to nothing but darkness. It is the same with many people who were once enlightened but now are stumbling in darkness because they did not guard their heart against pride.

Let us look at some of the effects of pride in us. It does the following:

1. **Deceives us:** "The pride of your heart has deceived you, you who dwell in the clefts of the rock, whose habitation is high; you who say in your heart, 'Who will bring me down to the ground?'" (Ob 1:3).

2. **Causes us to forget God**: "When your heart is lifted up, and you forget the Lord your God who brought you out of the land of Egypt, from the house of bondage" (Dt 8:14). Bear in mind that just because you believe in God doesn't mean that you haven't forgotten Him. You might remember Him in theory but in practice you have forgotten Him, "The wicked in his proud countenance does not seek God; God is in none of his thoughts" (Ps 10:4).

3. **Brings destruction upon our lives**: "The Lord will destroy the house of the proud" (Prv 15:25); and "Before destruction the heart of a man is haughty" (Prv 18:12).

4. **Blocks the answer to our prayers**: "Two men went up to the temple to pray, one a Pharisee and the other a tax collector. The Pharisee stood and prayed thus with himself, 'God I thank You that I am not like other men—extortioners, unjust, adulterers, or even as this tax collector. I fast twice a week; I give tithes of all that I possess'. And the tax collector, standing afar off, would not so much as raise his eyes to heaven, but beat his breast, saying, 'God, be merciful to me a sinner!' I tell you, this man went down to his house justified rather than the other; for everyone who exalts himself will be humbled, and he who humbles himself will be exalted" (Lk 18:10-14).

5. **Corrupts our ability to show true love**: "Love suffers long and is kind; love does not envy; love does not parade itself, is not puffed up" (1 Cor 13:4).

6. **Keeps God far from us**: "Though the Lord is on high, yet He regards the lowly; but the proud He knows from afar" (Ps 138:6).

In addition to the effects of pride in our life, let us look at some sources of pride:

1. **Religiosity**: Many believers become very religious and self-righteous after obtaining knowledge of and having experiences in the presence of God. They start to feel so holy that they look down on everyone else. This was the attitude of the Pharisee, "The Pharisee stood and prayed thus with himself, 'God, I thank You that I am not like other men–extortioners, unjust, adulterers, or even as this tax collector. I fast twice a week; I give tithes of all that I possess'" (Lk 18:11-12).

2. **Position and Power**: "Then Uzziah prepared for them, for the entire army, shields, spears, helmets, body armor, bows, and slings to cast stones. And he made devices in Jerusalem, invented by skillful men, to be on the towers and the corners, to shoot arrows and large stones. So his fame spread far and wide, for he was marvelously helped till he became strong. But when he was strong his heart was lifted up, to his destruction, for he transgressed against the Lord his God by entering the temple of the Lord to burn incense on the altar of incense" (2 Chr 26:14-16).

3. **Wealth**: "With your wisdom and your understanding you have gained riches for yourself, and gathered gold and silver into your treasuries; by your great wisdom in trade you have increased your riches, and your heart is lifted up because of your riches" (Ez 28:4-5).

Now, I know that as you are reading this you might be saying, "I wonder if I am a victim of pride?" Don't wonder; test yourself. Are you ready? Let's start...

a. Do you consider yourself to be better than other people because of your personal appearance, economic status, level of education, skin color, family background, etc.?

b. Do you let others' opinion of you hold you back from doing things?

c. Do you get angry and upset when people don't agree with your view?

d. Do you consider yourself to be always right?

e. Do you have trouble admitting your faults when you are wrong?

f. Do you look down on people on the basis of creed, position, personal hygiene, appearance, race, or ethnic background?

g. Do you find it hard to be impressed with other peoples' accomplishments?

h. Are you constantly trying to interrupt peoples' conversations to give your comments and opinion?

i. Are you constantly criticizing others?

j. Do you strive to impress others with your talent, wealth, physical appearance, athletic ability or professional ability?

If you answered yes to any of these questions, you could be a victim of pride. Here is what the Lord thinks of proud people: "Everyone proud in heart is an abomination to the Lord; though they join forces, none will go unpunished" (Prv 16:5). If you have sinned by pride, I encourage you to confess it and repent of it in the sight of God so you can continuously grow in your relationship with Him. Put on humility; it will reverse the effects of pride. We gain God's favor when we put on humility; then, He will assist us in our daily activities.

Our humility before God can even change God's mind:

> *But as for the king of Judah, who sent you to inquire of the Lord, in this manner you shall speak to him, "Thus says the Lord God of Israel: 'Concerning the words which you*

have heard-because your heart was tender, and you humbled yourself before God when you heard His words against this place and against its inhabitants, and you humbled yourself before Me, and you tore your clothes and wept before Me, I also have heard you,' says the Lord. "'Surely I will gather you and your fathers, and you shall be gathered to your grave in peace; and your eyes shall not see all the calamity which I will bring on this place and its inhabitants'" (2 Chr 34:26-28).

May the Lord continue to bless and keep you.

Let's Pray

Lord, vest me in Your humility so that my daily walk may be pleasing in Your sight, in Jesus' name I pray, **Amen**.

THE HEART...

The heart! The heart! The Bible speaks quite a lot about the heart and gives us instructions on how we should maintain it. Proverbs 4:23 exhorts us to "Keep your heart with all diligence, for out of it spring the issues of life." The devil knows very well that out of our heart the issues of life spring forth. This is why he works relentlessly to contaminate our heart with all sorts of atrocities. He knows that when our heart is full of hate, malice, grudges, pride, lust and jealousy, he will attain his goal to stop us from being blessed and seeing the glory of God in our daily lives.

For this very reason, it is of the utmost importance that we keep our heart pure and clean. This is the main reason the Bible tells us to guard our heart. We guard our heart by keeping a strict watch on what comes to us by our eyes, ears, etc. Along with this preventative measure, we need to ask God daily to clean our heart simply because none of us is perfect. The devil is well aware that malice, grudges, lusts, and the like in our heart makes us defiled before God. Defilement of our person not only puts us outside of God's camp, but also causes us not to stand in God's presence. Psalm 24:4-5 tells us that only "He who has clean hands and pure heart... He shall receive blessing from the Lord, and righteousness from the God of his salvation."

Therefore, if we desire to stand in the presence of God and be blessed by Him, our duty is to humble ourselves before Him on a daily basis and ask Him to search us and reveal our innermost thoughts and feelings. This is because our knowledge and understanding of the intricacies of the heart is not only biased, but very limited. To add to that, the Bible tells us, "The heart is deceitful above all things, and desperately wicked." It goes on to question, "Who can know it? It is only God who knows it. I, the Lord, search the heart, I test the mind" (Jer 17:9-10). This clearly shows that only God has the ability to indiscriminately search man's heart and reveal the things that so easily defile us.

Only God knows us inside out. So whatever He reveals as not good, our next step is to ask Him to give us the strength to remove it from our life. By doing this, we will continue to stand in His presence and be a testimony to His word, which says in Matthew 5:8, "Blessed are the pure in heart, for they shall see God!"

Let's Pray

Dear Lord, search my heart and help me to let go of whatever is in me that is not from You. Take away the heart of stone and give me a new heart that is pure and receptive to Your will, in Jesus' name I pray, **Amen.**

The Revolt Continues!

> *Then Hezekiah turned his face toward the wall, and prayed to the Lord, and said, "Remember now, O Lord, I pray, how I have walked before You in truth and with a loyal heart, and have done what is good in Your sight." And Hezekiah wept bitterly (Is 38:2-3).*

We must learn to live our lives with an attitude of revolt if we really want to conquer the promises of God. Many believers are living a life of shame, pain and anguish because they carry within themselves a passive spirit. In other words, they live their lives accepting everything as it comes, even when it is coming from the enemy.

The Bible clearly shows that the men and women God used to carry out His purpose were people who were spiritually aggressive. They knew how to use the power of "choose and refuse." Unfortunately, religion today has crippled many people's ability to fight for what is rightfully theirs in Christ Jesus. They teach that we must learn to bear our cross and be humble. It is as if they believe that when the Bible says we are to take up our cross and follow Him, it means we should surrender to defeat and mediocrity, or as if to be humble means to be weak.

This kind of teaching is wrong. God never intended for His children to live defeated lives. But unfortunately, if we don't learn to revolt–to fight for our rights, God Himself can't do anything for us because He cannot go against His own principle. God has given us the option to choose either life or death: "See, I have set before you today life and good, death and evil... therefore choose life" (Dt 30:15, 19). Even though God urges us to choose life so that we may live, it is still up to us to accept or reject it.

Dear friend, there is power in choosing and refusing. What you choose and refuse in this life has a lot to do with the kind of life you will have.

God created us to make a difference, but it is the spirit that is in us that determines whether we will be motivated to make a difference or be hindered in this life. There are many ways we can view this, but let us look at it this way— you can go to a dealer and buy a brand new car, one with a very powerful engine; but if you fill the tank with water

107

instead of gas, you will cripple its potential to serve its purpose. So it is with us. God created us in His own image and likeness and commands us to be the head and not the tail. But if we allow that passive spirit to enter and control us, all our God-given abilities will be crippled and we will never reach our potential in this world.

I strongly believe that the graveyard is filled with unfulfilled assignments, because those people allowed the spirit of passivity to control their lives. The Bible says, "The soul of the diligent shall be made rich" (Prv 13:4). In other words, an aggressive soul shall prosper. The righteous king Hezekiah knew that he had a mission to accomplish and he was not going to surrender to defeat even when God told him to "Set your house in order, for you shall die and not live" (Is 38:1).

Hezekiah refused to accept this word as final because his mission was yet to be fulfilled. He knew God had the power to do better and God was pleased with Hezekiah's attitude of revolt and aggressive spirit. Therefore, He changed His mind toward Hezekiah, healed him and added fifteen more years to his days.

How powerful this is. Suppose Hezekiah had not revolted; he surely would have died. However, he refused to die and chose to live. Now keep in mind that Hezekiah's bad news came from God, yet he refused it. Now, how many people are receiving bad news from the devil and are humbly accepting it. How painful this is! Jesus tells us that if we are born of God, we will overcome the world. He did not mean this only in the sense of temptation and sin, but I personally believe we will overcome in all areas and aspects of our lives. The world represents shame, poverty, defeat, misery, pain, suffering and much more. Our future depends on us because God will never force His blessings or his plans for our lives on us.

For God's plan to take effect in our life, we first have to be revolted and fight for our right to the good life He has promised us.

Now my question to you is, "What kind of spirit is in control of your life?" Hear the word Hezekiah spoke as he praised God for his deliverance: "For Sheol cannot thank You, death cannot praise You; those who go down to the pit cannot hope for Your truth. The living, the living man, he shall praise You, as I do this day; the father shall make known Your truth to the children" (Is 38:18-19).

Friend, in order for Hezekiah to speak in this manner, he had to revolt against the situation. You might never be able to speak like this if you don't revolt. God bless you in Jesus' name.

Let's Pray

Lord, help me to be humble to accept
Your will for my life and to be revolted enough
to resist all the plans of the enemy against me.
I pray, **Amen**.

THE POWER OF
THE WORD

Then they cried out to the Lord in their trouble, and He saved them out of their distresses. He sent His word and healed them, and delivered them from their destructions (Ps 107:19-20).

It is very important that as believers, we understand the power of God's word. The Bible tells us that God's word is His seed. But we must understand that in order for the life in the seed to be manifested, the ground it is planted in must be good.

Oftentimes, we get an unknown seed, and if we judge it by its appearance or how dry it looks, we might think it is dead and lifeless. But we would be surprised to know that the same seemingly lifeless seed, if taken and sown into good soil and watered carefully, soon will have life sprouting from it and become a tree that produces much fruit. So it is with the word of God when we hear or read it. Sometimes it might seem or sound lifeless. But if we provide good ground for it to be sown and take care of it, eventually we will see it producing fruit.

The ground is our heart in which we must plant the word of God. We must take care of it daily and watch over it lest the enemy come and steal it away. As we read in Psalm 107, God heard when they cried out for help and the answer came when He sent His word. As they received the word. They received their healing. There are many people who are constantly asking God for help, healing, deliverance, and more, but at the same time, they are always ignoring the word. The Centurion said to Jesus, "Send a word and my servant will be healed," and so it was – the healing was in the word. It is only when you receive the word and apply it in your life that you will see the results. One of my favorite scriptures is Isaiah 55:11: "So shall My word be that goes forth from My mouth; it shall not return to Me void, but it shall accomplish what I please, and it shall prosper in the thing for which I sent it."

God's word is powerful and is life to those who receive and believe it. Once it finds good ground, it will bring forth a harvest. I pray that you will prepare the ground of your heart for the word of God to be sown there. Then you will reap the harvest of His promises. God bless you abundantly, in Jesus' name.

Let's Pray

Dear Lord, help me to keep the ground of my heart ready for Your word,
in Jesus' name, **Amen**.

THE ROCKS OF LIFE

A story is told about a very wise professor who always sought to help his students understand the gift of life and that it must be lived wisely so God's name can be glorified through it. One day, as he began his class, he picked up a big empty glass jar and began to fill it with pieces of rock. He then asked his class if the jar was completely full. Everyone agreed that it was full. So the professor then poured a box of pebbles into the jar and gently shook the jar. The pebbles began to roll into the open spaces between the rocks.

He again asked the class if the jar was full. Of course, everyone agreed that now it was definitely full, and they began to laugh. The professor then poured a box of sand into the jar. Now the sand filled every bit of remaining space in the jar.

The professor then began to teach wisdom to his class by saying, "Class, I want you to know that your life is like this jar. The rocks represent the important things—God, your family, your health and anything that is very precious to you and brings glory to God. If any of these things were lost, you would be greatly affected. The pebbles are things like your job, house, car, etc. The sand is all the other things in life; the simple things that are not so important. If you put the sand into the jar first, there will be no room for the rocks or the pebbles and so it is with life. If you spend all your energy and precious time on the small unimportant things, you will not have room for the precious and important things of life."

What a wonderful lesson to be learned. Whenever we have our priorities out of line, we will always fill our lives with unnecessary things. These things will eventually occupy the place of the important and necessary things. I pray that as we continue to go through this life, we will be diligent in getting rid of sand from our lives to make room for the rocks, the solid and necessary things of life, so we can grow and be who God desires us to be.

Let us learn to pay closer attention to the things that are necessary for our happiness and our lives. May the Lord bless you in Jesus' name.

THIS IS THE WAY!

Your ears shall hear a word behind you,
saying, "This is the way, walk in it"
(Is 30:21).

Every day, people work very hard trying to find the way that leads to success and riches. But sad to say, many have died, or are dying, without finding even the slightest trace of success or riches. Even though this is so, many still head down that same road, as we will see in the following story.

Once there was a certain lady who became so frustrated at not being rich that she decided to obtain riches at any cost. So she started to run the race of the "get rich." One fine day as she journeyed along, a certain man approached her. Though he was rich, he didn't look like it nor did he look like he could help make somebody else rich. As they talked, he asked her where she was heading. She explained that she was on a journey to get rich. Upon hearing this, he gladly offered her the opportunity to become rich, for he was very rich. Because his appearance wasn't up to her expectation, she refused to believe him and would not give him a second thought. She turned him down.

Throughout the journey, she totally ignored him. He was equally determined to make her believe he could do for her what he said. He kept following her and insisting he could help her. As determined as he was, he soon found out just how difficult it was to convince her that he was in a position to make her rich. After quite a while, he was finally at his wits' end. It so happened that the weather suddenly changed and they both got caught in a very rough storm that eventually cost them their lives.

Those who knew the lady and the dream she had, took her body, buried it and wrote these words on her tombstone: **Died trying to get rich**. In the same way, those who knew the rich man, took his body and buried him next to her and wrote on his tombstone: **Died trying to give her riches**.

This story has a very sad ending as it happens sometimes in life. Like this lady, there are many people who, despite trying very hard throughout their lifetime to find riches, happiness, peace, etc., still die without accomplishing any of their dreams. The worst part is that they were all offered an opportunity that guaranteed they would achieve their goal, but they turned it down. On the other hand, just like that man, our Lord Jesus Christ also died. But He did not die trying to give us—He has already given it. It is in His death that we are enabled to achieve wealth, riches and much, much more. So there is no need for us to kill ourselves in an effort to gain riches. The voice of God is saying, "This is the way, walk in it." Though He speaks, many are out of tune to His voice and have not taken heed to His words. They continue to work themselves to the point of death. The death of our Lord Jesus Christ was not only for our salvation but to give us life and life abundantly and that is riches indeed! So let us hear Him and be fulfilled. If you are determined to be happy, you must be determined to hear the voice and words of the Lord. Jesus was so determined to give us this great wealth that it cost Him His life on the cross. So why shouldn't we hear Him and be happy?

Let's Pray

Lord, help me not to ignore Your words. I thank You, Father, for speaking to me today and showing me the way that I should walk, **Amen**.

TRUSTING GOD'S PROMISES IN YOUR WILDERNESS

So Abraham rose early in the morning, and took bread and a skin of water; and putting it on her shoulder, he gave it and the boy to Hagar, and sent her away. Then she departed and wandered in the Wilderness of Beersheba. And the water in the skin was used up, and she placed the boy under one of the shrubs. Then she went and sat down across from him at a distance of about a bowshot; for she said to herself, "Let me not see the death of the boy." So she sat opposite him, and lifted her voice and wept (Gen 21:14-16).

When Sarah demanded that Hagar and her son be sent away from her household, God spoke to Abraham, who was not willing to let his son go. God confirmed to him that because Ishmael was his child, He would bless him. So I'm sure when Abraham sent Hagar and her son away, he made them aware of the promises of God to bless the child. But the Wilderness of Beersheba washed the promise away from Hagar's mind. That is how the enemy wants us. He will always try to use our wilderness to make us doubt and forget the promises of God.

We must understand that just because God promises us something, doesn't mean challenges won't come across our path. No! For sure, there will be wilderness in our journey. At times, God allows us to face the wilderness to test our heart to see how much we trust Him and believe His words.

> *And you shall remember that the Lord your God led you all the way these forty years in the wilderness, to humble you and test you, to know what was in your heart, whether you would keep His commandments or not (Dt 8:2).*

But unfortunately, often when the wilderness comes across our path, we stop looking up to God and start to focus on the wilderness—the difficulties. That is why, like Hagar, many times we lose hope and settle for defeat instead of persisting to the end.

Abraham had given Hagar provision for the journey, and as long as the provision lasted, she was willing to keep going. When she ran out of man's provision, she was ready to quit. Be assured that when man's help ends, God is ready to take over. God never said the child was going to die; rather, He promised that he was going to be the father of a mighty nation.

God stands behind His words to see that they materialize. Isaiah 55:11 confirms this:

> *"So shall My word be that goes forth from My mouth; it shall not return to Me void, but it shall accomplish what I please, and prosper in the thing for which I sent it."* Another scripture tells us, *"God is not a man, that He should lie, nor a son of man, that He should repent. Has He said, and will He not do?" (Nm 23:19).*

God will not lie and not fulfill His promise to you. So when He promises you something, no matter what comes across your path, He will be there to help you through it.

Don't lose focus of His promises, remain steadfast. If your wilderness is talking about death, you must continue to talk about life. Overcome evil with good. There is a well in your wilderness provided by the God of your promise. It is there to sustain you on your journey.

Hagar had gone spiritually blind. Her problem robbed her of spiritual sight. That is why she couldn't see the well of God's provision: "And God heard the voice of the lad. Then the angel of God called to Hagar out of heaven, and said to her, What ails you, Hagar? Fear not, for God has heard the voice of the lad where he is" (Gen 21:17). While she was crying and expecting the worst, God sent an angel who asked her what was wrong. In other words, the angel wanted to know why she was in despair. What had become of the promise God gave her, which said, "I will make him a great nation" (Gen 21:18). Again, God reminded her of His plan for her son's life and restored her sight, her ability to see the caring and loving hands of God as He showed her the well. "Then God opened her eyes, and she saw a well of water. And she went and filled the skin with water, and gave the lad a drink" (Gen 21:19).

As you read this message, you may be going through some kind of wilderness. You are weary from the cares of life. You are burdened by worries about your financial life, your love life, the future of your children, or other concerns. The promise of God is slowly fading away from your heart and mind. But I encourage you now to fill your container in the well of God's provision and be strengthened in your inner man to continue the journey in Jesus' name. Remember, He who starts a good work in your life is faithful to complete it, "Being confident of this very thing, that He who has begun a good work in you will complete it until the day of Jesus Christ" (Phil 1:6).

Let's Pray

Lord, please help me to be mindful of Your words that say that You will never leave me nor forsake me. May I say, even as Your servant said, "Yea, though I walk through the valley of the shadow of death, I will fear no evil; for You are with me."
In Jesus' name, **Amen**.

TRUSTING THE GREAT PHYSICIAN

If you diligently heed the voice of the Lord your God and do what is right in His sight, give ear to His commandments and keep all His statutes, I will put none of the diseases on you which I have brought upon the Egyptians. For I am the Lord who heals you (Ex 15:26).

Many times, people have difficulty receiving the blessings of God because it sounds too easy. I remember one time praying for a lady who was in a lot of pain, and after laying hands on her and proclaiming her healed in Jesus' name, she laughed and said, "I didn't know it was so easy." But what we must understand is that there is nothing too difficult with God. As the scriptures put it, "For with God nothing will be impossible" (Lk 1:37).

When Jairus, the ruler of the synagogue, was told that his daughter was dead, Jesus said, "Do not be afraid; only believe" (Mk 5:36).

The Lord God wanted His people to know that He was their Healer, and I believe that He wants us to know that He is also our Healer today. He is the Great Physician. If we obey His words, He stands ready to show us His power. But there is something very important that every recipient of or candidate for His blessing must learn to do. We must not be moved by the voice or sight of our condition, but by what we believe.

If Jairus had been moved by what he heard or what he saw, he would have missed the miracle he needed in his life.

Faith is not seeing to believe, but believing to see. What you believe, you shall see. "Now faith is the substance of things hoped for, the evidence of things not seen. For by it the elders obtained a good testimony" (Heb 11:1-2).

Faith starts with believing God's character and knowing that He is who He says He is. It ends with believing God's promises and knowing that He will do what He says. The Bible says, "For by it the elders obtained a good testimony. Everyone who believes by faith will obtain a good testimony because God's promises never return to Him void. "So shall My word be that goes forth from My mouth; it shall not return to Me void, but it shall accomplish what I please, and it shall prosper in the thing for which I sent it" (Is 55:11).

So when the promises of God sound too easy to be true, understand that it is because of who He is. There is nothing that is too difficult for Him, "For thus says the Lord of hosts, the God of Israel: 'Houses and fields and vineyards shall be possessed again in this land'" (Jer 32:15). As the songwriter says, "Only believe, all things are possible, only believe."

Let's Pray

Lord, I pray that I will believe and not doubt, in Jesus' name, **Amen**.

UNDER OUR FEET

As a boy going to school, there was a boy in my class who was very big and strong for his age; we were all like ants beside him. But despite his size, he was constantly being beaten up by us. He was like a puppet in our hands. Now that I am an adult, I look back and realize that his subjection to us was not because of a lack of physical strength or capacity; it stemmed from mental weakness.

This weakness controlled him because a spirit of fear possessed him. As long as he was fearful, he could never realize that he was endowed with the strength and ability to defeat us. By not assuming his potential, he was being afflicted by us daily, although we had significantly less ability and strength. He found himself in quite an unfortunate situation. However, the story could have been much different if he had shaken off the fear and stood up to us from the very beginning. Certainly, he would have taught us a very good lesson. But thank God he didn't come to his senses until

I had already moved away from the school and out of the town. Ha! Ha! Ha!

Just like that young boy, we find many believers today living their lives in fear, despite the fact that they have all that it takes to move ahead and overcome in life. They have been endowed with the name of Jesus, His Spirit, His Word and great testimonies, yet they remain defeated. Fear has possessed them, and they become mentally bound and crippled by its effects. The songwriter says, "Emancipate yourself from mental slavery; none but ourselves can free our minds." How true this is. It is only when we fully assume our position in Christ, stand firm upon His promises, and use our God-given authority over situations and circumstances, that we will finally experience this freedom in Christ that is spoken of in His words, "Where the Spirit of the Lord is, there is liberty" (2 Cor 3:17). This clearly tells me that where the spirit of fear is, there is bondage.

Let's keep this one thing in mind—in life's journey, things are going to happen that try to instill fear in us. But having this feeling of fear does not change the fact that our God, who is strong and mighty in battle, remains as our light and salvation. He is there to protect and deliver us. So for whatever reason this feeling of fear comes, it is our responsibility to shake it off at once and free our mind of what the devil wants us to think. Only then can we truly confess just as the Psalmist David: "The Lord is my light and my salvation; whom shall I fear? The Lord is the strength of my life; of whom shall I be afraid?" (27:1). So let's stand up and assume our position in Christ and put fear where it belongs—under our feet!

Let's Pray

Dear God, in Jesus' name, help me in this moment to overcome all fear. I now renounce and rebuke the spirit of fear out of my life and bind it along with its bondage. I cast it out, never to return again in my life. I now assume my authority in Jesus Christ, **Amen**.

WHEN THE UNBELIEVER VISITS

And when the queen of Sheba had seen the wisdom of Solomon, the house that he had built, the food on his table, the seating of his servants, the service of his waiters and their apparel, his cupbearers and their apparel, and his entryway by which he went up to the house of the Lord, there was no more spirit in her (2 Chr 9:3-4).

Quite often, God will bless us believers in such a way that the news of His favor on our lives will spread far and wide. When unbelievers hear about our accomplishments, just like the queen of Sheba, they will want to come and see for themselves. Unbelievers are never content with just hearing; they always want to see before they believe, for they live by sight.

Now when unbelievers come near us, what impression will they get from us? When the queen of Sheba came to Solomon, she came with difficult questions. But the Bible tells us, "So Solomon answered her all her questions; there was nothing so difficult for Solomon that he could not explain it to her" (2 Chr 9:2).

The visit of the Queen of Sheba was not a threat to Solomon, but an opportunity to testify about the glory of God and His power. God blesses us so His name can be glorified through us. His desire is for us to be His testimony unto unbelievers. Many people have the idea that to be a good Christian we must be poor. But that is far from the truth. Some people will only acknowledge the power of God when they see it materializing in us. Of course, not everyone who sees the hand of God upon our lives will automatically convert to Him. But even if they don't, at least they will respect us and the God we serve.

Solomon humbly began by seeking God wholeheartedly. It was because of this decision that God blessed him with much wisdom and understanding. With this spiritual blessing, he was able to answer all of the queen of Sheba's questions. In addition, God had also blessed and prospered him greatly. When she saw how blessed he was, she was literally speechless:

> *And when the Queen of Sheba had seen the wisdom of Solomon, the house that he had built, the food on his table, the seating of his servants, the service of his waiters and their apparel, his cupbearers and their apparel, and his entryway by which he went up to the house of the Lord, there was no more spirit in her (2 Chr 9:3-4).*

At this point in Solomon's life, his house was in order. This is exactly what the blessing of the Lord does to us: "The blessing of the Lord makes one rich and He adds no sorrow with it" (Prv 10:22). The queen of Sheba, recognizing that his wisdom and prosperity stemmed from his connection to the God he served, exclaimed,

"Blessed be the Lord your God, who delighted in you, setting you on His throne to be king for the Lord your God! Because your God has love Israel, to establish them forever, therefore He made you king over them, to do justice and righteousness" (2 Chr 9:8).

She was moved to acknowledge the God of heaven, whose work was evident in the life of Solomon, simply by what she saw. As believers, it is important that we do not serve God with lip service. We must seek to honor Him with our lives so He can show Himself strong on our behalf. In that way, others can see and glorify His name.

Christians must not accept living a defeated life. Like Solomon, we must go before God and seek His face, His wisdom, His knowledge and His understanding to be all He desires us to be. In the beginning of Solomon's reign, he went before God in humility saying, "Now give me wisdom and knowledge, that I may go out and come in before this people; for who can judge this great people of Yours?" (2 Chr 1:10). As a result of his prayer request, he was equipped to surprise his unbelieving visitors. They had to acknowledge his God.

The problem that arises from receiving God's blessings is that we must watch our ways lest we fall into the trap of the enemy.

We cannot become so busy that we begin compromising our relationship with God, and end up like Solomon, who made that grave mistake in his old age:

> *But King Solomon loved many foreign women, as well as the daughter of Pharaoh: women of the Moabites, Ammonites, Edomites, Sidonians, and Hittites from the nations of whom the Lord had said to the children of Israel, "You shall not intermarry with them, nor they with you. Surely they will turn away*

your hearts after their gods". Solomon clung to these in love. And he had seven hundred wives, princesses, and three hundred concubines; and his wives turned away his heart. For it was so, when Solomon was old, that his wives turned his heart after other gods; and his heart was not loyal to the Lord his God, as was the heart of his father David (1 Kings 11:1-4).

Let's Pray

I take a stand against the spirit of poverty and lack. I claim God's blessings for my life. I will be a testimony unto others as they look and see what He has done in my life, in Jesus' name, **Amen**.

YOUR FAITH IN ACTION WILL STOP YOUR BLEEDING!

Now a certain woman had a flow of blood for twelve years, and had suffered many things from many physicians. She had spent all that she had and was no better, but rather grew worse. When she heard about Jesus, she came behind Him in the crowd and touched His garment. For she said, "If only I may touch His clothes, I shall be made well." Immediately the fountain of her blood was dried up, and she felt in her body that she was healed of the affliction (Mk 5:25-29).

There are many people today who are living a life of constant "bleeding." Bleeding in their health, bleeding in their spiritual life, bleeding in their finances and bleeding in their relationships. The reason why they are experiencing so much bleeding is because they have not learned to use their faith. They have what the Bible describes as "dead faith," which is faith without action. The Bible teaches us that in order for our faith to produce results, it must be accompanied by action. I have personally come in contact with good Christians who are living a shameful life because they have not learned to put the faith that comes from the word of God to work in their lives like the woman did in the scripture above. If she had exercised her faith twelve years earlier, she would have been healed twelve years earlier. But her lack of action kept her bound for those twelve years.

When we were saved, we were translated from the kingdom of darkness to the Kingdom of Light. This means that we no longer survive by the world's principles.

In the world, we lived by "sense knowledge," which is by our human ability. But in the Kingdom of God, we live by faith. In the world, we were limited by human ability, which means that we could hope to achieve only what was possible by human knowledge and ability. Anything beyond that was considered impossible, but not so in the Kingdom of God. When we put our faith into action, we can go very far and accomplish great victories in Jesus' name. For example, the woman with the issue of blood couldn't get the solution to her problem by human ability. But when she put her faith to work, the Bible says that the fountain of her blood instantly stopped. We know that this woman's faith was alive because it had action. We see her faith when she believed that if she could touch the Lord's clothes, she would be healed. We also see her faith in action when she left her house and acted upon her belief and touched His clothes.

Faith + Action = Results. It is only when you start applying action to your faith that you will see the fountain of all your "bleeding" stopped. "What does it profit, my brethren, if someone says he has faith but does not have works? Can faith save him?" (Jas 2:14).

May the Lord bless you abundantly.

$1.9 e

$6.39   11/5/ry

CPSIA information can be obtained at www.ICGtesting.com
Printed in the USA
BVOW04s0535250914

368230BV00005B/9/P